Spot the Difference

Flowers

Charlotte Guillain

Heinemann
LIBRARY

www.heinemann.co.uk/library
Visit our website to find out more information about Heinemann Library books.

To order:
☎ Phone 44 (0) 1865 888066
🖹 Send a fax to 44 (0) 1865 314091
💻 Visit the Heinemann Bookshop at www.heinemann.co.uk/library to browse our catalogue and order online.

First published in Great Britain by Heinemann Library,
Halley Court, Jordan Hill, Oxford OX2 8EJ, part of Harcourt
Education. Heinemann is a registered trademark of Harcourt
Education Ltd.

© Harcourt Education Ltd 2008
The moral right of the proprietor has been asserted.

Editorial: Sian Smith and Cassie Mayer
Design: Joanna Hinton-Malivoire
Picture research: Erica Martin and Hannah Taylor
Production: Duncan Gilbert

Printed and bound in China by South China Printing Co. Ltd

ISBN 978 0 431 19231 4

12 11 10 09
10 9 8 7 6 5 4 3 2

British Library Cataloguing in Publication Data
Guillain, Charlotte
  Flowers. - (Spot the difference)
  1. Flowers - Juvenile literature
  I. Title
  582.1'3

Acknowledgements
The publishers would like to thank the following for permission
to reproduce photographs: ©Corbis pp.**12**, **23 middle** (Craig
Tuttle), **5** (Scot Frei); ©FLPA pp.**20** (Foto Natura/DUNCAN
USHER), **14** (Minden Pictures/INGO ARNDT), **19** (Chris
Demetriou), **21** (Holt Studios/Nigel Cattlin), **23 bottom**
(Holt Studios/Nigel Cattlin), **6** (Nigel Cattlin); ©Getty Images
p.**10** (TAUSEEF MUSTAFA); ©istockphoto.com pp.**4 bottom
right** (Stan Rohrer), **4 top left** (CHEN PING-HUNG), **4
top right** (John Pitcher), **4 bottom left** (Vladimir Ivanov);
©Nature Picture Library pp.**8** (Andrew Parkinson), **15** (NEIL
LUCAS), **9** (Philippe Clement), **11** (Ross Hoddinott), **16** (Ross
Hoddinott); ©Photodisc pp.**13**, **22 right** (Hans Wiesenhofer);
©Photolibrary pp.**18**, **22 left** (Chris Burrows), **17** (David
Dixon), **7**, **23 top** (Pacific Stock /Dahlquist Ron).

Cover photograph of flowers reproduced with permission
of ©Photolibrary (Pacific Stock /Dahlquist Ron). Back cover
photograph of dahlias reproduced with permission of
©Photodisc (Hans Wiesenhofer).

Every effort has been made to contact copyright holders
of any material reproduced in this book. Any omissions will
be rectified in subsequent printings if notice is given to the
publishers.

Contents

What are plants?

Plants are living things.
Plants live in many places.

Plants need air to grow.
Plants need water to grow.
Plants need sunlight to grow.

What are flowers?

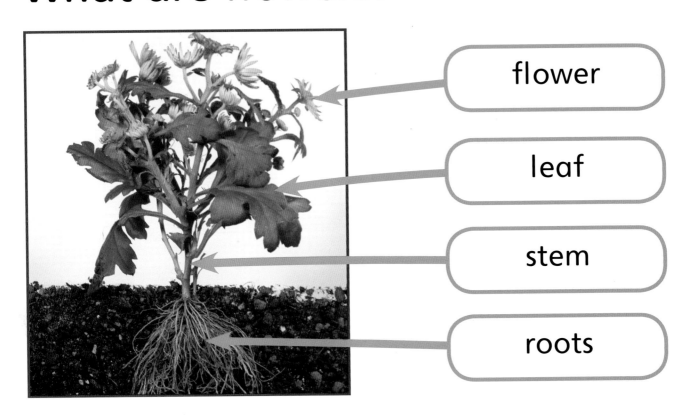

flower

leaf

stem

roots

Plants have many parts.
A flower is a part of a plant.

Many plants have flowers.

Different flowers

This is a poppy.
Its flowers are red.

This is a viola.
Its flowers are blue.

This is a tulip.
It has one flower.

This is a primrose.
It has many flowers.

petal

This is a foxglove.
Its flower has one petal.

petal

This is a dahlia.
Its flower has many petals.

Amazing flowers

This is a rafflesia.
It is a very big flower.

This is a titus arum.
It is a very tall flower.

This is a bumblebee orchid.
It looks like a bee.

This is a trumpet flower.
It looks like a trumpet.

This is a starflower.
It is a star shape.

This is a bluebell.
It is a bell shape.

What do flowers do?

Flowers make seeds.

Seeds grow into new plants.

Spot the difference!

How many differences can you see?

Picture glossary

 **flower** the part of a plant that makes seeds

 **petal** part of a flower

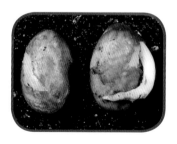 **seed** plants make seeds. Seeds grow into new plants.

Index

Notes to parents and teachers

Before reading
Take in a collection of different flowers. Talk to the children about the flowers and ask them to name the different colours. Show them the different parts of the flower. Let the children smell the flowers and talk about why flowers are often bright colours or have a strong smell (to attract insects). Talk about how the flowers need insects to take the pollen from one flower to another – this helps them to produce seeds.

After reading
- Place some flowers of different colours on a tray and show them to the children. Explain that you are going to cover the tray and take away one of the flowers. The children can guess which flower is missing.
- Show the children pictures of different flowers. Divide the children into groups of three or four and give each group a different flower. Ask some children to be insects and to fly around and visit the flowers. When they have been visited by an insect the children should sit down. Tell the insects that they must each visit two different flowers and they should touch the backs of each child in the group before the move to another group. See which insect visits the flowers the fastest.
- Make 3D flowers using different coloured tissue paper. Fold a piece of tissue paper (approximately 10 centimetres square) into quarters. Draw a petal shape starting from the folded corner and away from the open edges. Cut out the shape. Unfold the petals, pinch the centre of the flower and attach to a stick. Display the flowers in a jar.